First published in this format 2015

The Taunton Press
Inspiration for hands-on living®

The Taunton Press, Inc., 63 South Main Street,
PO Box 5506, Newtown, CT 06470-5506
e-mail: tp@taunton.com

Text and Projects: Kollabora
Photographers: All photos by Richard Vassilatos
© www.richardvassilatos.com, except for the step-by-
step photos by Scott Phillips © The Taunton Press, Inc.
Jacket/Cover and Interior Design: Kimberly Adis
Editor: Carolyn Mandarano
Series Art Director: Rosalind Loeb Wanke
Series Production Editor: Lynne Phillips
Copy Editor: Betty Christiansen
Model: Amanda Lynn Kim

Threads® is a trademark of The Taunton Press, Inc.,
registered in the U.S. Patent and Trademark Office.

The following names/manufacturers appearing in
Super Simple Jewelry are trademarks: Play-Doh®,
X-Acto®

Library of Congress Cataloging-in-Publication Data

Super simple jewelry : 11 modern, versatile pieces
to make in 30 minutes or less / Kollabora.
    pages cm -- (Threads selects)
  ISBN 978-1-63186-363-9
1. Jewelry making--Juvenile literature. I. Kollabora
(Firm)
  TT212.S87 2015
  745.594'2--dc23

                         2015019609

Printed in the United States of America
10 9 8 7 6 5 4 3 2 1

Contents

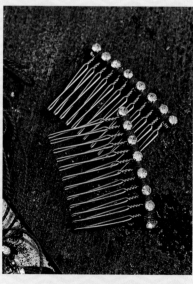

kollabora

Find more simple jewelry projects at Kollabora.com

MAKE FRIENDS

Lia Griffith

Ama Ryllis

Francesca Stone

Anna Sergeeva

LEARN SKILLS

Basic chain making

Assembling chains, charms, and pendants

Basic stringing and knotting

The root of Kollabora is "working together"—we unite makers, crafters, and DIY enthusiasts of all skill levels to get inspired, share projects, buy and sell PDF patterns, and connect with each other and their favorite brands.

At the forefront of the modern maker movement, our diverse online community of creative influencers includes some of the most well-known and innovative DIYers sharing high-quality, unique, and fashion-forward content from sewing and knitting to quilting, jewelry making, home décor, and more!

Join Kollabora for free to learn, get inspired, and share what you're making. Whether you're a novice or an expert, Kollabora is a great place to unite with other makers and share in the love for modern craft.

FIND PROJECTS

Small feather clay necklace
by Nora

DIY leather necklace
by Ama Ryllis

Leather wrapped brass jewelry
by Anna Sergeeva

Geode leather jewelry
by Lia Griffith

DIY enamelled faux agate rings
by Francesca Stone

DIY ring from paper leavings
by Anastasia

Tools and Materials for Jewelry Making

You don't have to be a pro to make stand-out jewelry you'll want to wear every day of the week! There are tons of quick and easy ways to make fun, versatile pieces using just a few tools and basic skills.

From reusing broken jewelry to making custom rings (it's easy, we promise), you'll be surprised at how many beautiful things you can make—no experience necessary!

In this booklet, you'll learn how to use basic tools and components to make jewelry; along the way you'll discover how to incorporate uncommon objects, how to use polymer clay, and how to measure for fit.

Check out the tools and materials on the next few pages.

Basic Tools

1	Crimp tool	**8**	Piercing tool or leather punch
2	Side cutters	**9**	Straight razor
3	Flat-nose pliers	**10**	X-Acto® knife
4	Needle-nose pliers	**11**	Painter's tape
5	Pom-pom maker	**12**	Stamp hammer
6	Plastic ring mandrel	**13**	Stamping block
7	Glue	**14**	Metal stamps

Basic Materials

1 20-gauge metal wire
2 Peanut chain
3 Metal hair comb
4 7-strand beading wire
5 38-mm ribbon crimp ends
6 Gold flat back earring posts
7 Silver earring posts with loop
8 Metal stamping blanks
9 Crimp beads
10 6-mm jump rings
11 3-mm jump rings
12 Small silver chain
13 Flat back rhinestone chain
14 Gunmetal chain
15 Box chain

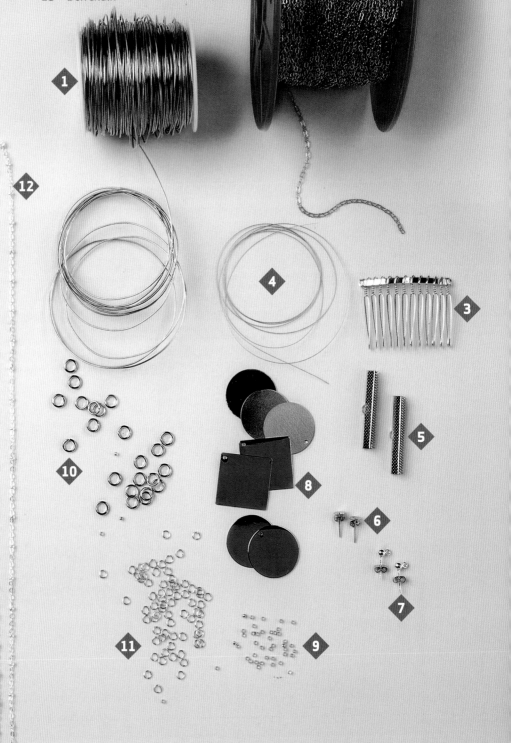

16 Embroidery floss
17 Polymer clay
18 Leather pieces
19 Beads (wooden, ceramic, plastic)
20 9-in. zippers

Leather Earrings

It's true that leather gets better with age and even more true that it never goes out of style. Mix and match colors and textures to create your perfect pair of earrings that are both edgy and timeless.

SKILL LEVEL
Beginner

TOOLS & MATERIALS
Leather scraps
2 jump rings
2 earring hooks
Scissors
Piercing tool or leather punch
Needle-nose pliers
Flat-nose pliers

TO MAKE THE EARRINGS

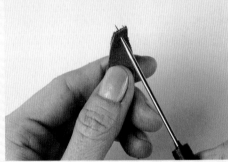

1. For each earring, cut 2 or 3 pieces of leather in various shapes. We used a long rectangle, a long triangle, and a short rectangle for each earring.

2. Use a piercing tool or leather punch to punch a hole in the top of one piece of leather. Attach a jump ring.

3. Place the second piece of leather underneath the first and mark the space to punch a hole. Repeat with the third piece of leather, then use your piercing tool to pierce holes in the 2 remaining pieces of leather. Layer your leather pieces in the order you wish and attach both to the open jump ring.

4. Using needle-nose pliers, attach the jump ring to an earring hook. Use the needle-nose pliers and flat-nose pliers to hold the jump ring and earring hook as you close the jump ring. Repeat steps 2–4 for the second earring.

Zipper Cuff Bracelet

Often the best way to inspire an interesting new jewelry project is to grab found materials and just go for it! Case in point: Who knew a short, chunky zipper could end up being such a statement-making bracelet?

SKILL LEVEL
Beginner

TOOLS & MATERIALS
1 zipper, 7 in.
2 ribbon crimp ends,
30 mm to 38 mm
1 jump ring
1 clasp and catch
(optional)
Scissors
Flat-nose pliers
Needle-nose pliers

TO MAKE THE BRACELET

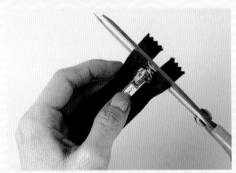

1. Trim the ends off the zipper on either side.

2. Place the crimp end on one end of the cloth and use flat-nose pliers to gently crimp it onto the material. Repeat on the other end with the other crimp end.

3. Open the jump ring using needle-nose pliers and slide both crimp ends onto the jump ring. If using a clasp and catch, attach the clasp to one crimp end and attach the catch to the other.

Tassel Necklace

This necklace has the look of a rare vintage find with a bohemian luxe appeal. Use found beads from a broken necklace or new ones to make a unique piece to wear alone or layered with your other favorites.

SKILL LEVEL
Beginner+

TOOLS & MATERIALS
Embroidery floss
for tassels
Beading wire
3 kinds of beads
in complementary
sizes and colors:
*1 strand of small
wooden beads*
*1 strand of
flat disk beads*
*1 strand of
bean-shaped beads*
Glue
Scissors
Side cutters

TO MAKE THE TASSEL

1. Wrap embroidery floss around 3 of your fingers to desired thickness (about 10 to 15 times).

2. Pull the floss off your fingers and hold at one end. Making sure to leave enough room to slide the tassel onto the wire, take the end of the floss and wrap it around the top of the tassel to secure.

3. Knot the end and use a dab of glue to hold. Let the glue dry.

4. Using scissors, snip the looped threads to create the tassel. Repeat steps 1–4 to create more tassels. We made 3 for this necklace.

TO MAKE THE NECKLACE

1. With side cutters, cut a piece of beading wire about the length of 1 arm. Slide your tassels onto the beading wire and pull them to the middle. Starting on the right side, add your wooden and flat disk beads in an alternating pattern until your work measures about 1¾ in. (or roughly 7 disk beads and 6 wooden beads). Repeat this step on the left side. On the right side, add your bean-shaped beads to measure 7½ in. (or about 20 beads). Repeat this step on the left side. On the right side, alternate your flat disk and wooden beads until they measure about 1½ in. (about 7 disk beads and 6 wooden beads). Repeat on the left side. On the right side, add wooden beads until they measure about 2 in. (about 18 beads). Repeat on the left side.

2. Tie together the 2 ends of the beading wire. Double-knot for security.

3. Hold the ends of the beading wire and thread them back through about 1 in. of the beads. Clip the remaining ends of the beading wire with side cutters.

Stamped Pendant

Minimalism with a kick: Stamp out what's on your mind and layer up these easy, delicate necklaces that are anything but basic.

SKILL LEVEL
Beginner

TOOLS & MATERIALS
Metal stamps
Metal stamping blanks
Stamping block
Painter's tape or washi tape
1 jump ring
1 box chain, in the length of your choice
Hammer
Needle-nose pliers

TO MAKE THE PENDANT

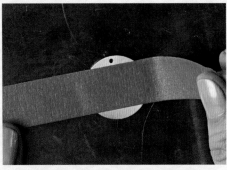

1. Choose the word or words you want to stamp and pick out your metal stamp letters. Tape your stamping blank to the stamping block using painter's tape or washi tape. Be sure the tape is placed over the area you'll be stamping.

2. Hold the stamp tightly in one hand, positioned on top of the tape and blank and with the letter indication facing you. Using a hammer, strike the stamp sharply about 3 times to mark the blank. Continue with other stamps until you've formed your word(s). Remove the tape and stamped blank.

3. Holding the jump ring with needle-nose pliers, loop the chain and stamped blank over the ring. Use the pliers to close the ring.

Wire Wrap Ring & Midi Ring

It's easier than you think to create custom rings and midi rings to stack on every finger. Because bare knuckles are so 2014.

SKILL LEVEL
Beginner+

TOOLS & MATERIALS
Narrow strip of paper, about 4 in. long
Tape
20-gauge metal wire
Ring mandrel
Side cutters
Flat-nose pliers
Needle-nose pliers
Nail file (optional)

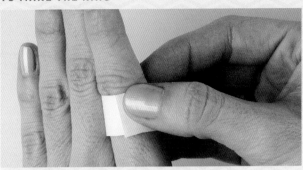

1. To measure your finger size, wrap a narrow strip of paper around the finger you want to wear your ring on. For a standard ring, measure to the base of your finger. For a midi ring, measure at the first knuckle. Mark the point where the paper meets with a pencil, then tape the paper to hold the size.

2. Slide the wrapped paper over the ring mandrel to determine your finger size.

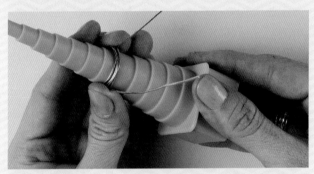

3. With side cutters, cut a piece of wire about 16 in. long and soften it by pulling it through your hands; this warms the metal and makes it more flexible. Place the ring mandrel in the center of your wire and bend the 2 ends parallel toward you. Position the mandrel so your ring size is centered on the wire, then begin wrapping the wire around the mandrel, working with the right side of the wire. Stop wrapping when about 3 in. remains. Pull the 3 in. of wire so it's facing you and parallel to the unwrapped wire. Wrap the wire on the left side around the mandrel, again leaving about 3 in. unwrapped. Bend the wire tails so they are parallel to each other.

4. Remove the ring from the ring mandrel. Place the ring lightly over your thumb and use flat-nose pliers to grip the ring in the center of the area facing you, making sure all layers of the wrapped wire are gripped by the pliers.

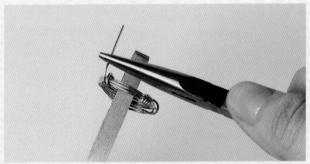

5. Grasp one wire tail with the needle-nose pliers and wrap it around the ring 3 or 4 times perpendicular to the layers.

6. Clip the remaining end of the wire you just wrapped with side cutters if needed.

7. Repeat steps 5–6 with the other wire tail, wrapping it around the layers. Use a nail file to smooth any rough edges of the wrapped wire if necessary. Use your needle-nose pliers to flatten the end of the wire against the ring.

Geo Clay Necklace

A subtle yet interesting mixture of abstract, geometric shapes and dainty chain make a decidedly art-meets-fashion statement.

SKILL LEVEL
Beginner

TOOLS & MATERIALS
Polymer clay
Beading wire
Small silver chain
Crimp beads
Rolling pin
Straight razor or
X-Acto knife
Piercing tool or
toothpick
Crimping tool
Side cutters

TO MAKE THE CLAY COMPONENTS

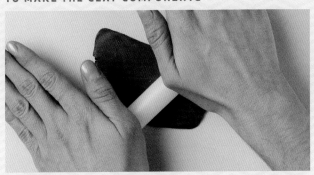

1. Rub the clay between your hands to soften it. Place the clay on a clean, flat surface and use a rolling pin to flatten it.

2. Use a straight razor or X-Acto knife to cut out your desired shapes.

3. Working with a small piece of clay, roll it between the palms of your hands to form a ball. Repeat to create the number of balls you want in your necklace. We did this twice, making 2 small beads.

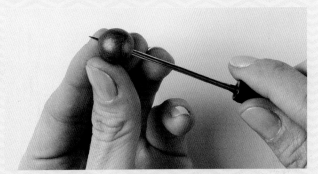

4. Use a piercing tool or toothpick to pierce completely through all the clay balls and shaped pieces. Bake the clay according to the manufacturer's instructions.

TO MAKE THE NECKLACE

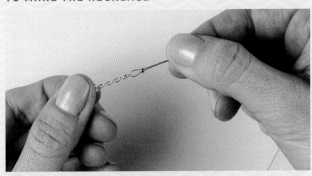

1. Cut a piece of beading wire about 6 in. long. Cut a piece of chain about 24 in. long. Thread the beading wire through one end of the chain.

2. Secure the chain using a crimp bead and crimping tool.

3. Thread the clay components onto the beading wire, then thread the remaining end of the beading wire through the remaining end of the chain; secure with a crimp bead, using the crimping tool. Thread the end of the wire back through the clay beads and cut the remaining end with side cutters.

Mismatched Clay Earrings

Create a range of fun, interchangeable earrings that will give you a different look every day of the week.

SKILL LEVEL
Beginner

TOOLS & MATERIALS
Polymer clay
Flat earring posts
(at least 2)
Rolling pin
Straight razor or
X-Acto knife
Side cutters or
scissors
Glue

TO MAKE THE CLAY EARRINGS

1. Rub the clay between your hands to soften it. Place the clay on a clean, flat surface and use a rolling pin to flatten it.

2. Use a straight razor or X-Acto knife to cut off strips of clay from the block, then cut out your desired small shapes. Bake the clay according to the manufacturer's instructions.

TO ASSEMBLE THE EARRINGS

1. Using side cutters or sharp scissors, cut down the side of the flat earring post.

2. Apply a dab of glue on the earring post, then place onto the back side of a clay piece. Repeat with the remaining earring posts and clay pieces. Let the glue dry.

Clay Bangles

Create tons of colorful bangles in all shapes and sizes to stack up and down your arms or mix with other bracelets to make your perfect look.

SKILL LEVEL
Beginner

TOOLS & MATERIALS
Narrow strip of paper, about 7 in. long
Tape
Polymer clay
Straight razor or X-Acto knife

1. To measure the size for your bangle, wrap a narrow strip of paper around the widest part of your hand. Mark the point where the paper meets with a pencil, then tape it together at the mark. You also can use another bangle for reference, using a measuring tape to measure the length.

2. Rub the clay between your hands to soften it. On a flat, clean surface, roll the clay back and forth with your hands, creating a long tube, as if you were rolling Play-Doh® into a snake.

3. Using the paper bangle or other bangle for reference, wrap the clay around the circle to measure the needed circumference. Be careful not to press too hard and distort the shape of the paper bangle.

4. Use a straight razor or X-Acto knife to cut both ends of the clay tube, making sure you leave enough clay to close the circle.

5. Gently push the clay ends together to seal the circle.

6. Support the bangle with one hand while using the fingers of your other hand to lightly roll the clay at the seam to smooth that section of the clay. Reshape as needed into a circle, smooth out any bumps or inconsistencies, then bake according to the manufacturer's instructions.

Chain Loop Earrings

Turn simple chain into a conversation starter that's modern and elegant yet casual. Add in different styles of chain to create your own unique look.

SKILL LEVEL
Beginner

TOOLS & MATERIALS
2 kinds of chain, about 6 in. each

Earring post with loop

Jump rings

2 pairs of pliers (needle-nose or flat-nose)

Side cutters

TO MAKE THE EARRINGS

1. Cut two 2½-in. pieces of one type of chain. Cut two 2-in. pieces of chain from the second type of chain.

2. Open 1 jump ring and slide 1 length of each type of chain onto the jump ring.

3. Attach the jump ring to the loop on 1 earring post, then close the jump ring.

4. Open another jump ring and slide the opposite ends of the 2 chains onto the jump ring. Attach an earring back to the jump ring, then close. Repeat steps 2–4 with the remaining 2 pieces of chain and earring post and back.

Clay Stack Rings

Thin, stackable clay rings create a cool, modern look with minimal effort.

SKILL LEVEL
Beginner

TOOLS & MATERIALS
Narrow strip of paper,
about 4 in. long
Tape
Polymer clay
Rolling pin
Straight razor or
X-Acto knife

TO MAKE THE RINGS

1. To measure your finger size, wrap a narrow strip of paper around the finger you want to wear your ring on. Mark the point where the paper meets with a pencil, then tape the paper to hold the size.

2. Rub the clay between your hands to soften it. Place the clay on a clean, flat surface and use a rolling pin to flatten it.

3. Using your paper as a template and holding it with the edge on the clay, cut out a hole in the clay with an X-Acto knife.

4. Using a straight razor or X-Acto knife, cut a square around the hole, making sure to leave enough room on the sides so the ring is sturdy. You can leave a straight edge along the bottom and top of the ring or cut diagonally across the top, but make sure the bottom is a flat line.

5. Repeat steps 2–4 to make more rings. Bake the clay according to the manufacturer's instructions.

Rhinestone Hair Comb

Upgrade your updo with rhinestone hair combs that add a touch of glam to your everyday hairstyles.

SKILL LEVEL
Beginner

TOOLS & MATERIALS
Metal or plastic hair comb
Flat back rhinestone chain
Glue
Embroidery floss
Sewing needle

TO MAKE THE HAIR COMBS

1. Using a thin line of glue, adhere the flat back of the rhinestone chain to the hair comb.

2. Wrap embroidery floss around the comb and chain, weaving it in between the rhinestones.

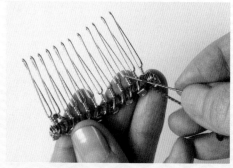

3. Tie off the end of the floss at the back of the comb by using a sewing needle to thread the end back through the wrapping. Make sure to also thread the beginning of the embroidery floss through the back to secure it. Cut the end of the thread. Add a dab of glue to secure the floss end if needed.

If you like this booklet, you'll love everything about *Threads*.

Read *Threads* Magazine:

Your subscription includes six issues of *Threads* plus FREE digital access. Every issue is packed with up-to-the-minute fashions, useful techniques, and expert garment-sewing advice – all designed to help improve your skills and express your creativity.

Subscribe today at:
ThreadsMagazine.com/4Sub

Discover our *Threads* Online Store:

It's your destination for premium resources from the editors of America's best-loved sewing magazine, designers, and sewing instructors: how-to and design books, videos, and more.

Visit today at:
ThreadsMagazine.com/4More

Get our FREE *Threads* e-Newsletter:

Keep up with what's current – the latest styles, patterns, and fabrics, plus free tips and advice from our *Threads* editors.

Sign up, it's free:
ThreadsMagazine.com/4Newsletter

Become a *Threads* Insider:

Join now and enjoy exclusive online benefits, including: instant videos, favorite articles, digital issues, pattern database, fun giveaways, and more.

Discover more information online:
ThreadsMagazine.com/4Join